JOGGING IS IN, SNOOPY

D1392151

**Also by the same author,
and available in Coronet Books:**

Jogging Is In, Snoopy

Selected cartoons from THE BEAGLE HAS LANDED Volume 1

Charles M. Schulz

CORONET BOOKS
Hodder Fawcett, London

Copyright© 1977 United Feature Syndicate, Inc.

First published by Fawcett Publications Inc., New York 1980

Coronet edition 1981

British Library C.I.P.

Schulz, Charles M.
  Jogging is in, Snoopy.
  I. Title
  741.5'973   PN6728.P4

  ISBN 0–340–26667–8

Printed and bound in Great Britain for
Hodder and Stoughton Paperbacks, a
division of Hodder and Stoughton Ltd.,
Mill Road, Dunton Green, Sevenoaks,
Kent (Editorial Office: 47 Bedford
Square, London, WC1 3DP) by
Cox & Wyman Ltd, Reading

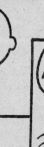

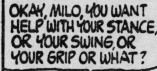

WHY AM I SITTING HERE IN A BOX IN THE RAIN?

BECAUSE THOSE TINY LITTLE KIDS NEED ME, THAT'S WHY... THEY THINK I'M A GREAT COACH...

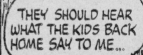

THEY SHOULD HEAR WHAT THE KIDS BACK HOME SAY TO ME...

"HEY, CHARLIE BROWN... DON'T LET YOUR TEAM DOWN BY SHOWING UP!"

HEY, MANAGER! I'M MAKING OUT OUR LINEUP...SEE WHAT YOU THINK..

I'VE GOT SCHROEDER DOWN FOR CATCHER, LINUS AT SECOND BASE AND SNOOPY AT SHORTSTOP...

➤

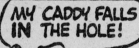

HERE'S SOMETHING ELSE TO THINK ABOUT..

DO YOU KNOW WHAT FRANCIS BACON SAID ABOUT READING?

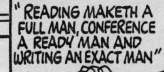

"READING MAKETH A FULL MAN, CONFERENCE A READY MAN AND WRITING AN EXACT MAN"

THEN AGAIN, WHAT DID SHE KNOW?

SCHULZ

→

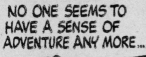

HITTING BALLS AGAINST THE GARAGE MUST BE GOOD PRACTICE...

IT'S PROBABLY ALSO FUN, ISN'T IT?

UNTIL SOMEONE PARKS THE CAR!

OKAY, "PARTNER."

LET'S GET A FEW THINGS STRAIGHT... I HATE TO LOSE!

I'LL MAKE ALL THE LINE CALLS AND TAKE ALL THE OVERHEADS! ALL YOU HAVE TO DO IS GUARD YOUR ALLEY!

AND JUST ONE SMART REMARK ABOUT MY FAT LEGS GETS YOU A KNOCK ON THE NOGGIN!!

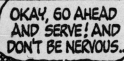

SEE THAT FAT LADY OVER THERE?

SHE'S THE MOTHER OF ONE OF THE KIDS WE'RE PLAYING....

SHE COMES TO SEE THAT HER LITTLE DARLING GETS GOOD CALLS! SHE HATES ME

SHE KNOWS THAT WHEN I'M PLAYING, ALL THE CALLS ARE GOING TO BE IN CENTIMETERS!

SECOND BOOK OF KINGS... CHAPTER NINE..

JEZEBEL IS SITTING THERE LOOKING OUT OF THE WINDOW, SEE...

BEFORE SHE CAN DO ANYTHING, THREE MEN PICK HER UP AND THROW HER OUT THE WINDOW!

SOUNDS LIKE A GREAT TV SERIES

MY UNCLE JUST GOT A PROMOTION

OH? WHAT DOES HE DO?

HE'S A DESIGNER FOR AN AUTOMOBILE COMPANY

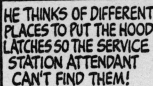

HE THINKS OF DIFFERENT PLACES TO PUT THE HOOD LATCHES SO THE SERVICE STATION ATTENDANT CAN'T FIND THEM!

COME ON ALONG, MARCIE

WE'LL GO OVER TO THE COUNTRY CLUB, AND GET JOBS AS CADDIES.. WE'LL MAKE A FORTUNE

I CAN'T TELL A PAR FROM A BIRDIE, SIR...

THOSE ARE BOWLING TERMS, MARCIE..DON'T EMBARRASS ME!

WHAT ARE THE LADIES ARGUING ABOUT, SIR?

MRS. NELSON WANTS STROKES, BUT MRS. BARTLEY WON'T GIVE HER ANY...

THIS IS VERY IMPORTANT BECAUSE THEY'RE PLAYING FOR A DIME-A-HOLE...

DON'T GIVE HER ANY, MA'AM!

IT'S NONE OF YOUR BUSINESS, MARCIE!